WALKABOUT

Trees

Henry Pluckrose

KU-248-958

FRANKLIN WATTS
LONDON•SYDNEY

There are many kinds of plants.
There are grasses, flowers,
shrubs and bushes
and trees.

30119 023 439 088

WALKABOUT

Trees

This edition 2003

Franklin Watts
96 Leonard Street
London EC2A 4XD

Franklin Watts Australia
45-51 Huntley Street
Alexandria
NSW 2015

Copyright © 1993 Franklin Watts
Editor: Ambreen Husain
Design: Volume One

All rights reserved. No part of this publication may be
reproduced, stored in a retrieval system, or transmitted
in any form or by any means, electronic, mechanical,
photocopy, recording or otherwise, without the prior
written permission of the copyright owner.

A CIP catalogue record for this book is available from
the British Library.
Dewey Decimal Classification Number: 582.13

ISBN: 0 7496 5262 4

Printed in Hong Kong/China

Photographs: Heather Angel 4, 28; Bruce Coleman Ltd
(G. Dore) 7, (F Futil) 10, (P Mortimer) 12, (P Clement)
15, (E Potr) 17, (H Reinhard) 20, 21, (B Coleman) 20
inset, (E Crichton) 21 inset, (G McCarthy) 25; Eye
Ubiquitous (K Mullineaux) 16; Chris Fairclough
Colour Library 14 inset, 23 insets, 29; Frank Lane
Picture Agency (Silvestris) 5, (R Wilmshurst) 9 inset,
(E & D Hosking) 11, (D Robinson) 27; NHPA (S
Dalton) 24, (E A Janes) 31; Oxford Scientific Films (H
Taylor) cover, (K & D Dannen) 8, (G A Maclean) 22;
ZEFA 9, 13, 14, 15 inset, 23, 26.

Additional photographs: Chris Fairclough

LONDON BOROUGH OF SUTTON LIBRARY SERVICE	
02343908 8	
Askews	Dec-2004
J582.16	

But what is special
about a tree?

A shrub or a bush
has leaves, flowers
and branches . . .
just like a tree.
The branches of a
shrub grow straight
from the soil.

A tree grows from the soil
from one single shoot.
This shoot is called
the trunk.
Branches grow from it.

The trunk and branches
of a tree
are protected by bark.
Bark keeps the tree
cool in summer
and warm in winter.
It stops the tree
from being dried by the sun.

As the tree grows,
the bark splits, cracks
and falls off.
There is always new bark
underneath the old.

There are many kinds of tree.
Each kind of tree
has its own special shape.
Some trees, like the English oak,
are tall and rounded.

Some, like the Atlas cedar, are shaped like a triangle.

Some droop . . .
as though they were sad.
This tree is called
a weeping willow.

Some are straight and slim.

All trees have leaves.
Some trees keep their leaves
throughout the year.
These trees are called
evergreen trees.
The evergreens which grow
in cold countries
have spiky leaves.

Some trees lose their leaves
in the autumn.
These are called
deciduous trees.
Most deciduous trees
have broad, flat leaves.

Leaves help produce
the food on which trees live.
Roots carry water and
chemicals
from the soil to the
branches and the leaves.

Each leaf contains
a green pigment
called chlorophyll.
The water and chemicals
sucked up by the roots
mix with the chlorophyll.
When sunlight shines on
them, the leaves make sugar.
Sugar is the food
which the tree needs to live.

You can identify trees
by their leaf shapes.
Some leaves are triangle-shaped,
some are long and thin,
and some are quite feathery.
What tree has a leaf
which is hard and prickly?

Beech

Mountain Ash

Oak

Holly

Birch

Maple

Hawthorn

Sweet
Chestnut

Willow

Alder

In springtime,
trees have flowers.

Without a flower
there could be no fruit.

Inside each fruit
there are seeds.
A new tree could grow
from each of these seeds!

These all grew on trees.
Do you recognise any of them?

Many kinds of living creatures make their homes in trees. Animals often live around the roots.

Insects live beneath
the bark . . .
and provide food for birds.

High above the ground, squirrels are safe from their enemies.

Birds build their nests in holes in tree trunks and in the forks of branches.

When a tree is cut down,
you can see the pattern of rings
in the trunk.
It takes one year for
each ring to form.

When the small branches have been cut from the tree, the trunk is sawn into planks.

Wood is used for
many different things . . .
for building houses,
for furniture, tools,
toys, boxes . . .
and even paper.
Can you think of
other things that wood
is used for?

Would you like to live in a world without trees?

About this book

Young children acquire much information in an incidental,
almost random fashion. Indeed, they learn much just by being
alive! The books in this series complement the way in which
young children learn. Through photographs and a simple text
the readers are encouraged to comment on the world in
which they live.

To the young child, life is new and almost everything in the
world is of interest. But interest alone is not enough. If a child
is to grow intellectually this interest has to be harnessed and
extended. This book adopts a well tried and successful
method of achieving this end. By focusing upon a particular
topic, it invites the reader firstly to look and then to question.
The words and photographs provide a starting point for
discussion. Discussion also involves listening. The adult who
listens to the young reader's observations will quickly realise
that children have a very real concern for the environmental
issues that confront us all.

Children enjoy having information books read to them just as
much as stories and poetry. The younger child may ignore
the written words ... pictures play an important part in
learning, particularly if they encourage talk and visual
discrimination.

Henry Pluckrose